SUNLIGHT IN
A CHAMPAGNE GLASS

Selected Recent Titles of William Oxley

Poetry

Collected Longer Poems 1994
Reclaiming the Lyre – New & Selected Poems 2001
Namaste: Nepal Poems 2004
London Visions 2005
Poems Antibes 2006

Anthologies

Completing the Picture (editor) 1995
The Sonnet at the Millennium (with Patricia Oxley) 2000
Selected Modern Poets of Europe
(translations; editor, with Patricia Oxley) 2004

Prose

Working Backwards – A Poet's Notebook 2008

William Oxley

Sunlight in a Champagne Glass

Rockingham Press

Published in 2009 by
The Rockingham Press
11 Musley Lane,
Ware, Herts SG12 7EN
www.rockinghampress.com

British Library Cataloguing-in-Publication Data

A catalogue record for this book
is available from the British Library

ISBN 978-1-904851-29-5

Printed by the MPG Books Group
in the UK

Contents

ROOMS

Acknowledgements

Acknowledgements and thanks are due to editors of the following who published some of the poems in this volume:
Acumen, Agenda, Ambit, Chapman, Chimera, Dream Catcher, Envoi, Equinox, Littoral, Markings, Other Poetry, Poetry and Audience, Poetry Ireland Review, Poetry Nottingham International, Poetry Salzburg Review, Quattrocento, Retort, Scintilla, Seam, South, Stand, Temenos, The Formalist (USA), The French Literary Review, The Frogmore Papers, The Herald Express, The London Magazine, The New Writer, The SHOp, The Spectator, The Wilfred Owen Newsletter, Timbuktu; and on-line *Three Candles* (USA), and www.falconeditions.com; and to Rockingham Press who published 'Morning in Antibes' and 'An Orange Tree' in *Poems Antibes*, and to Hearing Eye who published 'So You Write Poetry?' in *In The Company Of Poets*.

Opening Gambit

The sea
with its wide white paws
scratching terracotta sands

The sea
smelling of iodine, brine,
dishevelled green hair the rotten
toiletry of mermaids

The sea
its lamentation of shingle, its cries
and roars, that speaks to us
in the innermost night
of our unthinking selves

The sea
that is the great white bird
of pure presence whose right eye
is the sun, and left the moon,
that threatens to drown us
in an awesome love, a great death.

To address it
is to begin talking to God.

Noticing Is Where We Start

Going daily to the beach for years
you get to notice certain things –
the way in spring or summer waters
are like a crystalline web that sings,
and rocks grown smooth as skulls
white powdered and dusted for prints;
or the pebbly sands where wild gulls
cavort and the odd child madly sprints.

Yes, notice boats, especially papery yachts
that cross the horizon like pop-up ducks
in a shooting gallery, or what rots
in sullen crevices: everything that unlocks
this secret life of which all are a part.
Noticing may not be believing, but it's a start.

A Home

The sea like a fabric
sun-lit and wind-wafted,
the shore a broken line
of time-exploded rock;
and many a heart thumps
at the sight alone:
uplifted or depressed
half-recalling a home
a place perhaps witnessed
before it was born.

Herring Gulls

Among the herring gulls
every conceivable sound
of suffering's found:
birth cries, conception, murder –
a screech and screech-whimper
that pierces the wildest wind
and runs along the nerves of the sea.

Fishwife choruses of complaint,
the restless critics of a town;
birds-of-the-real
like journalists of decay,
even when the sea's at rest
there's no respite from your
sensation-seeking in tide and muck.

Why not now and then shut up
and let the dawn and dusk alone?
Must you always remind us
survival, too, like every state
has its own special sounds,
its natural music
and a bitter harmony?

Ghost Boat

(photograph of an old Brixham Trawler)

Trawling monochrome seas of the past,
old boat you occupy memory now:
tall sharp-sparred mainmast
with sky-stitched rigging through which
hoarse winds shrilly blew.

Your salt-starred crew with chapped hands
and rum-ripe faces are gone:
asleep in wormy bunks on land
beneath earth's huge bulkhead undisturbed
by ocean's roll and rhythm.

In photography's album of lost days
I find you pictured in deathlessness
caught in the act of braving bold waves,
and it is as if you still sailed on
past tussocky headlands of time.

Foam sudding your sodden sides, voices
calling tarry commands,
tired arms tugging at mainbraces –
events in the deaf-and-dumb language
of image, you frozen trawler

tossed forever in the bay of my mind!
And I cannot help asking how real
is the past? Or death, how blind?
When an old boat that is now no more
can sail still by my living shore?

Light on the River Dart
(for Neil & Shelley-Anne)

Light on the Dart
Light in the dark
It strokes the masts
And water going past.

Day is champagne
Dusk a darker wine;
Goes down the minted sun
And a shilling moon comes up.

On gently jogging boat
Our each mind floats
A cork on its own river
Separate but together.

And with daylight gone
Lights of all come on
In houses beading hills
Mirroring inner glow until
Light on the Dart
Is light in the dark

Six The Mount Sonnets

1.
Rockery of heather, geraniums, sun running
over it like spilled juice. Solid brawn wall.
Every new summer the poetry again stunning,
remembered, re-read, each word magical
with feeling. Something writes here in flowers.
Long ago taken up by love and love of sea
I restlessly search this place for new powers
of intensity. Let words of lost years come to me.
My garden in Torbay an evilless Eden
become lit by a deathless radiance
and those yachts that glide by make a scene
of far, unearthly, whispered transcendence.
And terraces of stone, elderberry, fence posts, show
we may actually know what we want to know.

2.
Glassy-eyed day of winter, indecorous
in its dullness. I stare into it and beyond.
My house says an eternal wind licks us,
and looking I am listening; also feel its hand
that parts the bay's waves to make white flowers
on blue. The ragged allotments touched by frost
are a comforting shanty town where old growers
who have spent their lives 'like lost',
feel they can get back to basics, nature.
I am, of course, not sure of this: *speculatum*.
But what else drives seeding nurture
but a rapture better than dying, keeping *stumm*?
Success comes to few, but all need it.
And gardeners, simple folk, can grow it.

3.
What is the air but a scarf of smells?
Dead mackerel, salt on breeze like
star-grains, odour of dying leaf that falls
onto late cut grass, sweet sweat of night,
light-licked lichen and herbs that spice,
the rare and subtle body odours of trees
that give, like roses, olfactory life to space;
and earth by which everything finally breathes.
Air is what the artists cannot paint
nor live without. It is the score sheet for sound.
Panting lover, gasping athlete, praying saint
do their business here where music is found –
air, the one thing unseen from my window,
a shapeless invisibility that lets all grow.

4.
Let us reify the things of mystery
in Devon, that was once of Broceliande
Forest where Druids turned Christian eventually
and poets celebrants of ordinary things to hand:
a holy grail at the heart of everything.
Once Merlin was here, Arthur's enchanter,
and Taliessin whose destiny it was to sing
of cosmic things in days of wild dark winter;
become the stars' troubadour when the sun
was on soft roads of summer that ran
from Cornwall, Lyonesse to Byzantium;
and his song was of woman, his song of man,
giving ideas a sweet compulsive shape,
teaching love, and from fear effecting escape.

5.
Everyday the sea blossoms for Torbay,
tossing bouquets of itself at an ornamental
coastscape: villa'd, palm'd, and flower-gay.
How describe it? A mind/spirit temperamental?
A grey horse at morning, sun its shiny saddle;
at evening clouds treading its purple grape.
Its broad sweep of ideas will baffle.
Best to know it through each intricate shape,
however small, the naked foot finds on shore –
detritus of powder stone, brown kelp, torn
crustacean, pop-eyed, salt-spurned bladder-
wrack; and all else born to be reborn
through its atrocious erosion in whose mirror
reflects its many ambiguities of horror.

6.
Shall I suppose this view all an act? Untrue?
This beloved elderberry that gifts fruit
and shade; the mostly docile sea docile blue;
the pencil-shaded Dartmoor that makes one intuit
an art of hills; the hyaline view of sky
in water; dancing, twisting clouds – cloaks
of cold, smoke-like rain; birds like the shy
turnstone, or awful herring gulls loud
as fishwives – are they all what they seem?
Or is it, that here in this terraced Mount,
my 'window on the world' there is no gleam
or plan that time will yield, or thought surmount?
Impossible to believe that no good sense
can come of this: its beauty merest nonsense.

Just One

Come, let us lie down together
a short time in the mud
and love will make it forever.
Never mind the rats and blood
and everyday diseases of reason,
in truth life has but a short season.
Lie down, love, in the body's
fading beauty, your hair
to me, lips and hands, all
will be perpetually fair;
not one thing will ever pall
despite this cold, damp life of envy
and unjustness. Though dark
is always near and heavy,
yet there are stars starring the black;
and though mouths choke with tears
at all the polluted ways of days,
long since we blended our two fires
to make one blaze that stays
even the cold shiver of death's
breathlessness. So come, let us lie down,
now, and for always, just one.

Somehow Comforting

Quiet November day, tugging wind
sporting with lost leaves of lost seasons,
was to him like a return to true England.

Quiet purposeful sound of it: a day
of rivers somewhere, a bird or two,
and sawing and hammering in the distance.

Distance not great to the eye like shut grey.
Mud, too, was everywhere he saw,
in the bottom of woods, paths, and

churned-about, turned-over fields.
Rain fell and smoked and was cold,
pools grew blind and very still.

Landscape ached with dead time,
but it was only the settling
of vast decay. And something resisted.

A wild life under all that goes on
bedraggled as a rat in wet sedge
or a late flower gulping a moment of thin sun.

After the city with its grinding and sitting
this countryman's England, potato-dull
in November, was somehow comforting,
like a walking away that was towards.

Strangeness of Wind

Today is a good wind, a clean wind, a wind without travail.
It somersaults the headland and prods the dragon swell
of a smoke-grey bay. A good wind, a clean wind
that courses down from moor to sea and mind.

It finds its way into words, singing
through invisible grasses, whispering little shells of meaning
that litter the human shore. A wind of wit,
an irony pulling at leaves and dust that

insists we see and feel things lost or never there.
But like bellows it also blows up fair,
with hidden mouth, yesterday's embers that give
fresh form to dawn and what in the world it warms to love.

Wind that shapes and haunts and never leaves this coast –
a western wind, a flying force, a kiss, a ghost
that plays around the rocky edge of bitterness
in strange ambiguities of happiness.

St. Michael of the Rock
(Brentor, Devon)

On a surge of grey rock
sewn onto Dartmoor green and gold,
a militant fist of God, this old
church supplies spiritual shock –

a fierce gesture under blue-dyed
sky. A leafless tree veins the view
and birds are few – few
or none on this spare hillside.

Fourth smallest church in England,
hymned by constant wind
the climb to it is hard, unkind
to worshippers – some hand over hand

in worst winter weather. More alone
than souls it serves like mine,
it wakes the eternally sublime
in God's wildscape, once our home,

now the lost view of any tomorrow.
But whatever it is that has gone
of one thing I am resolved upon:
not to give way ever to sorrow.

Seasons

Autumn's flames of light and leaf
suggest decay and memory's grief;

Winter comes in ice-long breaths
leads to talk of painful deaths;

but Spring unclasps the frigid hand
and love spreads green about the land;

then Summer soon, or even late,
will now insist we celebrate.

Winter in a Canadian Suburb

In a posh Canadian suburb
where the cold is cold enough to
keep icebergs alive the wind-chill factor
plays the highest notes
violining the local trees.
Yet a joy, unaccountable, scuds
and skips around the awakened heart,
that secret rose in the dark interior
of body. Joy, the thud
of human separateness, found again
beyond every pain whatever, or weather,
found again in a frost-coloured suburb
that is home and not home but superb
in the lingering wind and indelicate cold.

THE KAHNAWAKE POW-WOW

1.
Driving and Arriving

Over the bridge in an automobile's ticking interior,
over the deep St. Lawrence, water-muscular,
great grey waters rippling by like a dream
under a cloudy, fishbone sky
adorning the skin of God's tepee, adored wigwam.

Down along mini-suburban streets,
little shacks, colour-bright as mock bungalows,
with rough notice boards edgily offering
cigarettes, tobacco, smokers' contraband –
the First Nation people's economy a smoking Quebec.

Driving on in a gas-guzzling Dodge
to find some rolled-out land, park space
of withered riverside grass, dust and trees,
poor trees, weak trees, trees of no account
living, quietly dying in noonday haze.

And there the tents and tepees, shacks and stalls
of a fête – to celebrate the Kahnawake Pow-Wow,
a festival that wears its subjugated air
in hungover mornings on the Mohawk Reservation
where trees protrude like the bones of myth
from a landscape lapped by leaden waters.

2.
At a picnic table

Two guys, one discussing some bright-nippled squaw,
feathered, the whole of the Wilderness in his voice.
Smooth-skinned face, wearing soft buckskin,
his hair lanky grey, most handsome man,
compelling, an Indian trapper and trader who
talks of deals and furs, a hunter of arctic fox,
bear, and the badger-like raccoon. And women.

His companion and auditor a slob in a
big hat, wearing a white t-shirt, who turned
eyes like black bullet holes of hate on...everyone.

This morning in the dusty, Mohawk Reservation,
the Indian trader said, 'Kinda think I'd like to settle down'.
A small breeze stirred in the shouted encampment,
a breeze that registered surprise at the man's words.

3.
'Renewing our spirits
through the power of the drum.'

A rigged-up arena of scaffolding and planks.
Powerful Indian women stewarding with walkie-talkies
preventing camera-snapping of sacred stomping tribal dancing
braves whose souls shall not be stolen,
braves like rainbow eagles in the dust
feathers waving coloured by nature's perfect palette.
Children and women too in the solemn jerking dance
uttering vocables of formalized shriek, cries
of lovemaking and death, to the deep throb of drum
thrashing loins, aching hearts, calling up
Algonquin wilderness of bears and ancestors of the totem,
compelling gods, the thump of whose spiritual silence behind,
is blind atavism of an alien culture to most spectators.

To the Mohawks, as to all Indian tribes, the eagle
is animal god, carved on every stacked totem pole –
its spirit summoned by the power of the drum:
displaying great pinions it soars, inspires,
and into the rocking air of invisible worlds
to which men and women aspire, it leads
where the great sky of imagination like a sunset bleeds.

Sun

The sun is death
This held-to-be source of light
and life is death.

Nothing has ever lived
there: no astonished witness
of its magma flowers

no young girl to
rush breathlessly through its burning fields
joyfully. No

loving at its million degrees
centigrade, heat
on its dripping arms

its coppery face.
Back turned to it
look for that realer sun

that never harmed a single star.
It is the sun of the mind
its light imagination. Immutable.

Numinous

The glass weeps in this window
near Waterloo Station
and coldly hisses on rails
that loop away to Surbiton

or elsewhere. Nowhere so ugly as
in rain, bedraggled bushes of town,
buildings leaking and looking
their age, skies that are down-

cast. But there is something numinous too,
shiningly implicatory
in the out-there of roofs and streets.
Like the mad whisper of history

it floats out and up from shapes
even of shops: edging along walls like a cat
its creeping luminosity of
how and why and what.

Sticking Point

A long way off from the politically toxified
crawling computer-calcified rooms
coughing their bland punditry
superior as ex-smokers

A long way from the troubling brilliance
of graduates of gain, fame
and kudos I never could
compete with, sleep with, love

A long way into the twilight of ambition
closer to the unpoisoned freedom
that circles cities and landscapes
and is just mind and sky, sky and mind

A long, long way that is away towards
the prospect of paradise
where the human sun is honest
and knows it is 'I am', and what

A too far for the pettifoggers who ache
for success but not,
so help me green, for those
who stick out for something more,
for flowers of light

That Very Private Thing

*'The major poetic idea in the world
is, and has always been, God ...'*
— Wallace Stevens

They search among words like rubble
for that very private thing
which would make perfection
in this warm room orange as summer,
while outside years pass like a canal
behind black railings of history.

Seven poets and a reader,
chewing mouthfuls of words, eating
and drinking, celebrating
the Mass of Life at an ordinary table
beside french windows. Outside,
London its stone-grey skies
and clouds, like words, are part
of the same perennial puzzle of making.

Seven poets and a reader
tinkering with texts
like mechanics tuning vehicles
or musicians making sound magic
fingering this and that.

Among the sprawl of the domestic
sofas, chairs, plants' whispering
greenery, poets meet:
a coming together of the human
to search the rubble of words
for that very private thing
which would make perfection:
that varied impeccable star we long to name.

No Poet of a Western Sensibility

There was no poet here
        of a Western sensibility
in the white unremembered hills
        invested with yaks and flies
and the sad, sad peasants amazed
        by time's shortness, being
in love only with the blank everest of eternity.

Spittle of blizzards erasing mountains
        enormous glaciers aching,
years of the yeti and snow tiger
        worshipped in monasteries of sky.
Loveliness was composed of stars and stars' death
        and only their poets knew of a motion
beyond speech and the very lightest breath.

Lammas Land

A form of customary generosity
like house-sitting as wealth-sharing.

'Land that was private property
till Lammas Day (August 1st)

but thereafter subject to common
rights of pasturage till the spring.'

It takes dredging of dictionaries
to tell the faithless this now.

Thinking of the excitement-quickened poor,
lice-licked, getting their hands on gold

for that was what pasturage then was –
feed the cattle and the kids for free!

Lammas: bread-and-mass. Break the word
into holy syllables as poets do,

or did when singing was the main thing
and festival made of harvest gold,

and celebration meant consecration
not worship of celebrity.

Feel true simplicity of ownerless earth,
golden age temporarily come again.

I really like the idea of Lammas Land
and shall see it from now on, on

every cattle-feeding field around
where tractors rut and crows tumble

generous skies and suggestive landscapes.
Feel it again, this lost benefit-in-kind.

Turnstone

This morning I watched a turnstone,
plump, brown and white turning stones
along the sea-frazzled,frizzled shore,
quite indifferent to me. Both of us alone,

little thin-legged thing, friendly as hell
is not. Over with the stones, humped lumps
to its darting beak, out no doubt
with quivering insects a bird could see well

but I could not. And just that moment
was our everywhere for bird and me,
with me thinking that grey, laundered day
was made suddenly, by a neat bird, innocent.

Venezia Futura

A poet took over Venice's indoor cafes.
Misremembering a line by Koch I am reminded
of our yellow sugar time of sweet April in Venice,
1973, when we lazed and loved, talked
and hoped for a better future for poetry than
the stringy Parnassus of coming post-modernism
or what chuffed the mainstream mainline in an old express
driven by Captain Larkin and chums.
                    In the taken-over cafes
by the shot-silk lagoon we wasted the air
in talk; or as tourists chatted-up pigeons
in San Marco ... carried that cafe life out
like a bright intellectual shawl among frugal trees
of the Lido washed on its less populous side
by an emerald Adriatic swimming in late tawny light.
Literature was still literature then, and poetry
a hard talk of beauty and standards
in Harry's Bar, Montins, and cobbled courtyards where
the ghost of Shelley raved like a wolf out of platonic woods.
                    Drunken gondoliers slept at late night tables
as we talked on in a dream of poetry and youth
(we were heart by heart there, had each other off by heart)
wine was our ichor and books ambrosia as Blake kicked
open doors so we saw how the low lapping canals
sucked the green moon and licked up stars
for us, and the slow drilling rain on wonky pavements
was the remorseless fertiliser of future inspirations.
                    Out of waterlogged Venice, that cold-breasted city
of moneyed gold and sea-swallowed rings, I had learned to speak,
speak to the stars, the wind, to blue-green earth
wandering patient-eyed in indefinite space.

Venice was my past in encapsulated moment,
a late, slightly ridiculous childhood; but out of it,
because of it, in the person of a
grizzled bohemian poet, and a lovely wife
I found my future as others their faith.

The Dance of Detail

It is love and death make
us poets, the wind that whirls,
the once-green wood that flakes,
the lovely hand that slowly gnarls.

It is the dance of detail
makes the ugly beautiful,
the sick and slavering light
of dying sun is nightly beautiful

as the dead black walls of
cities crack, reveal their miseries
and mysteries. To day's dirt
poets bring a love and make

patterns in death's ashes,
configuring with impulsive care
glow-worm words to add
something to something already there.

Remembering Kathleen Raine

My father in the grey gone years
when I was green
would say, 'Any man who claims
to understand women is a fool!'
Even so, I would have liked
to have understood you
a little better than I did.

       After all,
I knew your poetry well as any
having read all you wrote;
understood your proud platonic vision,
that temenos of the mind's temple
where stars circled like endless prayers;
and your poetry of northern isles
that captured the pure lamental note:
voice of wind and wild seals' sea
pounding shores of the rowan tree.

       Soul of art
and truth and poetry! So strange
the way you would entertain with
kindness, vision, hope, despair -
tea and oatcakes and whiskey hospitality
in your elegant London room.
But then turn a cruel face on youth,
belittle friends and authors
you had never read, puzzling me –
and, no doubt, those revenant angels
you so often spoke about.

       Sometimes
I felt Chelsea your true deserted shore

34

not the ravenous sands of western isles
where you had lost your love.
And all that wonderful scholarship
with your 'master' Blake, with Yeats,
Plotinus and dozens more seemed
just, in the end, a scholarship of bitterness.

          Why?
And further, why did you, mixer with royalty,
high academics and the famous, you
whom so many called a snob,
turn up for my birthday party?
          I'll never know.

Yet in quiet moments like now
I'll call back the jumbled calm
of your Georgian den-cum-drawing-room,
you with your flickering smiles, blue eyes,
and sun streaming past afternoon windows
like the glory of that
sought-after changeless intellect,
your wonderful talk taking me
back to creation's ancient springs.
You the Sibyl of Stanza Square*
as I once dubbed you, a presence
among presences teaching a divine wisdom
you claimed this age had lost forever.

          Now
you have gone on that final journey
to the greater understanding you craved,
I do not mourn you as much as miss you,
and as in life so in death
I remain, well, intrigued by you.

* *She lived, in reality, in Paulton's Square, Chelsea.*

The Vividness of Death
(i.m. Michael Donaghy)

The vividness of death came on me
in the place, a huge Islington chapel;
it burned and boiled so even shadows
were consumed. But words did not swell
they were dry, only sometimes lively,
poignant as in the mouths of widows.

Not old, the stricken poet was dead;
a musician too of banshee airs
that were sharp as unoiled gales on
mournful hills: an agreeable man celebrated –
his life, his work, his self now gone.

Poems read, words said, music played
and all in a dusty, secular spirit;
no deity invoked (even Mammon) and none prayed
for the poet's soul (which was a soul of wit).

Under the vast cupola many mourners
with half-held breath contemplated death.
The place was labyrinthine, a stone mind,
it was all corridors with shadowy corners
and separate halls and rooms to find
with bars and stage, dance floors and
in that strange building like a rubic cube of God
a danse macabre to an Irish band.

Highland

I see a mountain like MacIntyre's
Ben Dorain, almost
a lost mountain.
(It is, for it's
a mount of paradise).
All the unvisited years hang about it,
not mist but like an unending
summer day, honey-coloured, spun
with white glen water. A whisky mountain
thrust up by holy lochs,
those sprites of blue lakes
photographic clear, beautiful –
a frozen song of hills.

But its reality under cloud-cuffing
and winds from a throat of ice,
is that of astringent rocks, balding grass,
purple bog-heather, and possessed
of a sense of apartness like a
desert. It's a god-place,
a magical Highland ben, pibroch-riven.
Yet, even on a pretty calendar,
I can see its form of stillness
like that of an anteroom to dreams,
a water-coloured waiting room of death.
The spare, painful beauty where you
recognize the finite intermitted,
something that is not altogether of
this dimension, like love, like love.

A Little Poem

I wanted to write
a little poem
with intensities
of love and God.

Not a poem
of high abstraction
nor solid reality
of brute stone

but of cherishing
like sea cherishes
the shore sometimes,
and I you always.

Then I recalled
how we sought flowers
this blue spring,
cyclamen, bluebells

harmless burning in
undergrowth, with
orchids, celandines
and fading violets,

cowslips and stitchwort
adorning earth's
spread tablecloth:
coloured stars all.

And that was the poem
ready written
to remember by,
remember us by.

Like an Angel

(i.m. John Gurney)

1.

The desert like an endless pancake.
High above it, where I never was before,

I was locked in a long steel airbus:
life suspended animation, a bore.

Why do I think of it now, stars put out
one by one in dawn, blue coming more

and more, and fire running at the rim
of a great pan? Why? I can't be sure.

But stuck up there in my ignorance,
quite unaware you were no more

it comes back to me from time to time
your death, and the indifferent engine roar –

while far below were Arabian sands
and a paintblue Gulf washing a yellow shore.

2.

Funny, John, I should have been
where I was – see above (above!) –
when you died. You a flier, too,
in the R.A.F. that left you a poet:
two things that finally came together.
A flier with the look of an angel,
a poet whose mind was like Rilke's
always half among angelic orders.
But a damaged angel, too, a Coleridge
seen through the darker eyes of Hazlitt.
You wrote of cot deaths and death camps,
of the beauty of birds and butterflies,
mixed a world of horror and love
with trembling waters of divinity.
A new Blake and half-mad aviator
flying, writing, praying and hoping
by the seat of your pants as good pilots do.

What I'm trying to say, John, as I scribble
these few lines for you, is I haven't forgotten
you, though I missed your funeral,
your death because, funnily enough, I was
where I was: high in the endless sky
which I think is all of your mind now.
Or as you would have it: sky of
angels, elohim, God … and now you!

Old Poster

(i.m. Ken Smith)

Finding this old brown poster
twenty years spat out by time since
it came to me. Kept rolled with others,
still fresh as new varnish:
Ken serious, seriously
into his cowboy mode then –
as he was at those lit-chattering
parties in socialism's shagged-out
Conway Hall – a Wild West figure like
the past in the present.

Gypsy's got her globe of dreams,
faces in snow to peer at,
Ken had his bottle of wine.
The future was, he saw,
everyday apocalyptic –
cities in melt-down mode,
love lost easy as money.

The waters streamed blue-
and-white flocculent
behind the small boat he used
to ferry our brilliant bay.
And Dartmoor could be seen
beyond palms and sun-scrubbed villas:
cloud-black moor of rain
where the wind whistled over
bog-cotton, mire and tor
forever and forever
like the thin troubling line of eternity –
that horizon always there
to remind of shared beginnings.

Meeting Jon Silkin on
the Banks of the Salzach

A modest evening mild as dreaming
and a few polite stars coming over mountains
we met you, Jon, on a last sight-seeing tour
of Salzburg. 'Taking the air,
before taking to the air!' you punned.

While water swirled by and sucked
under darkened bridges, lovers hugged their
benches, and pretty lights tree-slung
vied with far away hanging planets,
you talked, venerable, leonine in the half-light

of the unique conference we'd just left:
generous time given over to the doings of the Muse
in our time. Little did I think
as we stood beside that wide glacial river
still kindly gentle in the darkling autumn light,

it would be the last small gossip of our life
with you, fair-minded dedicated poet
and friend. Now, a year on from that last
editing of every poet's work, I think of you
huddled in a noisy bar fingering

one half-pint of weak beer, rejecting wine
and whisky, whispering of what 'the bloody medics say'.
Low-voiced but still alert, I think you guessed
your spool of life was running out. But none could believe
it true. Soon though I and a thousand others were forced to grieve.

For a death, yes, and something more, for one
who served the tribe of poets and served it well.
So let me return this poem to where it began:
to a swift-smooth river wetting both its banks
for one remembered poet like a flood of thanks.

On Castle Cary Station
(i.m. Martin Blyth)

Twilight's blue, rich-fretted with
              incandescent gold, was soon to be
absorbed in star-lyrical night,
              moon-buttoned and lonely

yet lovely too as all memories
              of the once warm-lived dead.
The frost furred fields and bitter bite
              of wind brought to a sudden head

two lives not free of sorrow,
              grieving for a genial man
too wise for ambition but not despair
              who made the best companion.

Yet we on that chill platform were
              also content to be among those most
missing him, like his wife believing
              he was only gone, not lost.

A Face like Robert Graves'

His, 'sad-dog-face' she described it,
that battered, noble demeanour.
She, a fine poet of real wit,
I, Graves' long time admirer.

In the farmhouse he'd retreated to
in the rigours of World War Two,
at Galmpton, he'd managed to renew
life with a new wife, one true

enough to stay with him to the end. Now she
in Torbay's annual poetry week
has died, just as the civic society
raised a blue plaque to meet

the demand for things commemorative,
our modern museum-mind's need.
But nothing so captures, dead or alive,
as a phrase: 'sad-dog-face' indeed!

A few words and there he is
taking a glass in the Manor Inn
or scrambling the olive terraces
at Deya with a face like ... like sin?

God, guilt and virtue he wrestled,
poems and prose he gave us;
on the battle-field he sabre-rattled,
in peace preferred the Muse to Jesus.

So by his own words is he judged;
and judged by other's words too.
And like all men open to be misjudged.
But once en-worded nothing he can do.

Made not Born

Once, a lifetime ago, you knew a poet
    by what he or she wrote.
Now, my friends, it's not so simple,
    so plese take note.

There's no role for the gifted amateur,
    the aspiring Edward Lear;
though still poorly paid, poetry's
    now a professional career.

In every town or city, even village halls,
    tyro Byrons, teenage Keats,
newish Hughes and neuro-Plaths
    are being taught to ignore the Beats,

the Movement and onion-flavoured Martians,
    and trust instead to a fashion-tutor,
expert in networking, name-dropping,
    and composing by computer.

Of course, for the older person, it's too late,
    to become a 'poetry name' –
Arvon or no Arvon, pensioners
    will not enter its Hall of Fame.

But given youth and a little competence
    the way to become a poet is
no difficult thing these days –
    just pay your fee to some poetry biz

that runs a creative writing course
    and once you've learnt its ways with words
it will certify your talent is great
    and only the sky's the limit for you and birds.

Yes, it's a nice road to Parnassus now
    where criticism's weeds don't grow,
and sooner or later, there's a book and award
    when you've learnt to know who to know.

Nude Man Running

Yesterday, a nude man zigzagged
Goodrington's orange sand and green seaweed,
running and prancing with a boy's joy
towards the far cold tide and low sea
urged by laughter, whistles, hoots
of his holiday mates, and ceaseless gulls
that nothing amaze – not even death.

Naked and hirsute, lion-maned as an
all-black sunflower, he danced through indifferent
breeze and disapproving gaze, an unsubtle
streaker only the subtle sea could halt
covering genitalia with frozen fig-leaves of cold –
silver and wind-carved from water
in grey filtered light of an aqueous Eden
with its cloudy, always coy English sun.

So you write Poetry?

'So you write poetry?'
he made it sound like something
the police could get you for.
'Well, what's the use of that?
Let me tell you something –
most people can do it
and rhyme it as well,
which you don't seem able to do.

'But back to my question:
what's the use of it?
Can it win wars?
More likely lose them!
Of course, you'll say it's about love?
Well, I expect women like it.
But where's the money in it?
There isn't any, I can tell you!
And where's the fame?
None – unless you're dead
and what use is that?
Better be a footballer or politician
or a really criminal criminal,
if it's fame you want.

'No, let's face it, poetry won't
unstop a blocked drain,
start a broken-down car,
fix a bust washing machine,
cook a decent meal,
cure any sort of illness,
win you a bet on a horse,
keep you out of trouble
(though it might get you into it!).
It's just a hobby and

a funny one at that, I'd say.

'In fact, it's a waste of time
and that's harmful
for time's money and time's life
and neither should be wasted,' he concluded
turning on the television.

There is an England

There is an England I see every day
a figure at the far end of Autumn's road
or that time by the snow-white lake in Surrey.
Tradition's accumulative ghost abroad

on the soft hills of Somerset
or whispering in sudden turns taken
through the time-worn ways of London –
grey-eyed Islington, greener Camden.

There is an England of high skies
and low skies, of love and wit,
an England of us and world words
an England that is itself and I love it

as it quietly moves down history
(it's in no hurry) treading on prejudice
injustice, and never forgetting that sea
which made it what it is.

An island of light in a sombre sea
where races mix and melt, vanish
and come alive again through a tongue
of grandeur and compassion called English.

'The Sporting Pink'

The newspaper was northern pink
like words on a sheet of hopeful sky:
my dad would read it by the sink
and only now I wonder why

calling up that tough old learned man.
Nicknamed 'The Sporting Pink' it came
on silver Saturdays when every man
was armchair-based about the home,

checking Pools, raking fires, helping out.
It now comes back to me: those Pools
and horses were what it was all about.
Long gone my days of infant schools,

of wild weekends in fields and epic gardens
and kicking footballs in the foggy gutter.
Age it is that blinds and burdens
but there was a man who 'loved a flutter'

as he loved his son, and held to this:
'We are but flies to some malignant fate,
but should it not prove true
a bob or two will make an easier wait

until we really know.' But although since then
I've waited too to find out what's what,
have never found that any game
has ever brought me luck or not.

The Man from Somerset

A man stopped me while out walking
(September coolness and boats in the harbour
under wet air). He wanted to tell me,
'I'm here for a week's holiday, no longer...'
'You've missed the best of the weather.', I said.
'Couldn't come no other time, see,
I had to work all through the zummer –
seven days a week – to get shoes shipped
to America. Don't want 'em no other time, see?
Besides, th'company I works for be Quakers –
an' they don't think nothin' o' workin' all the time!'
The boats talked at their moorings below the hill
while the stranger chained me gregariously,
told me about his dog some motorist had nearly killed,
'Ran right over the brute 'e did:
Wurn't thinkin' 'bout what 'e wur doin'!
An' now the dog sometimes falls down
when it's runnin' like, but don't hurt itself, mind,
just collapses and gets right up again.'
I stared at the black nervous creature, grass-sniffing:
it looked none the worse for having been 'run right over' –
as respectable a canine specimen as the next, I thought,
hiding its much-licked wounds like many a human would.
Then the man told me he had, 'Worked
as a coal-miner in Somerset,
afore takin' this job in the export o' shoes, see!'
And I said I hadn't known there were any coal mines
in that sweet county more famed for cider?
'Nor be there now. But there wur afore
they gone and closed 'em...an' I worked there.'
I wondered who 'they' were, and had a sudden

image of subterranean fields lying stone-black
beneath apple-juicy orchards lapped in green...
But when I told the stranger I was 'a poet'
(he did ask), it brought a quick end to our talk,
and left me bemusedly thinking
how a man stopped me while out walking –
and it somehow mattered.

The Swallows

Catapulted across the outdoor table
where the champagne bubbled
the swallows came, tornadoes of feather,
straight to a gap above the shed's green door.

At breakfast, lunch or in the
coming Welsh twilight the swallows
worked their noiseless maths
of accuracy into an entertainment,

as four of us lazed the golden-tongued
weather. Shot through our languid talk,
blue-pencilling our words, they
excited the long hot days of summer.

In that briefly borrowed garden
with its rockeries of overheated flowers,
these birds twisted and turned in air,
dipped wings like fighter planes, privileged

us as avian lords who flew faster than
time: at first by-passing us humans
for that hole in the hut their exclusive home,
before settling forever in my mind.

Once

(i.m. Jackie Brown
1909 – 1971)

There was this old man, there often
when we went to school on the red bus
through smoke grey Manchester mornings.
Old man 'doing the bins' as was said,
waste bins at bus stops, in the park,
anywhere wherever there was one
on a beat between old Blackley,
Harpurhey and Collyhurst. Called
a down-and-out then, a tramp,
like a stubbled leaf under Autumn
or brown paper off a parcel. His
was the hour of the Dole waiting for
opening time in the long brown pubs.
                    As he nudged his way
like a dog with no sense of smell
past lampposts, shops, life,
dad's words fell about my awed mind,
'He was once a world boxing champ. Once.
Look at him now?' And look I did.
But couldn't see enough of him then.
                              Or now.

Death of a Specialist

Used to shuttling the stratosphere,
a Jumbo man, world-renowned specialist.

Up among the clouds
like cream cakes in a blue pan,

this medic from Chicago belonged to the world.
Only met him once,

but read his books – some style!
Mad about baseball and

fighting Parkinson's disease.
Sleek competitor

in gold-rimmed spectacles:
epitome of the top-flight.

Clever, suave, generous as
only money can enable.

Professional who drained brains
to get at the truth, enemy

of every goddam virus. Finger
on every pulse save his own?

Blown away at sixty by a heart attack,
the clinical silence deepened.

Winter Suburb in The Hague
(i.m. James Brockway)

Everything stripped gothic naked
especially the trees. Sky sucks up tears,

tears from eyes in a glass wind.
Boxing Day silence hollowed out

by occasional footsteps. In gabled houses,
solid apartments are families

crouching for meals, T.V., or games.
A stern formality dominates lives

and living spaces, the streets exude
both boredom and mystery.

What mystery? That of theatre and dream.
These streets are low guignol

an outdated set awaiting macabre actors:
one can still hear clatter of Occupation and Death.

But a lighted tram passes beyond trees:
a blur of beauty, a going on forever

in this period-piece suburb of locked-in lives.
Where there has been love even death gives way.

Delft

The largest windmill in the world?
At a roadside of snarling cars
beside the long clank of tramlines.
the high symbol of the Low Countries,

its flailing sails and boring stonework
flaunts it: something of history,
but like so much its time now gone.
The largest windmill in the world?

Dykes groan at the weight of water,
the truculent sea somewhere snivels
and canals are everywhere watery wounds.
Solid Holland of flat fields and cheeky tulips.

One day in Delft is enchantment.
A blue and white world painted on porcelain.
Gilded town hall. Squares. Aroma restaurants.
Delft at the Dutch end of civilization:

a land of futile frontiers and freedom.
Something worthy. Something solid. Something dull.
Delft like a glazed china dish
under a grey sky. Empty and breakable.

Café Mythos

That's Deucalion over there, the old guy
with adjustable stick, says it's a caduceus given him
by Hermes. The solid, white-haired matron in
an apron's his wife – yes, you've spotted 'em –
-the couple talking to those other geriatrics
Baucis and Philemon – I'd call 'em all the Saga Lot
but it'd hopelessly mix myths. As for that tall beauty
with the sun-bronzed cleavage, draped round the end
of the bar, sulking over a cigarette,
smoke swirling round her golden head,
that's Sappho, staggeringly attractive if
a touch butch. But see him next the fireplace?
That pale faced fop, hair gilded grey and
shadows under eyes, lovely cheekbones though
but smudged with deeper shadows still, debauched
now, once handsome like that modern poet
whatsisname? Not Ovid, not Orpheus, not Bertram Bilious –
-can't just think of the name but done in, almost
as dodo as Dylan Thomas – well, he's,
believe it or not, Paris son of Priam king of Troy.
His fellow royal Aeneas is here somewhere too.
Well, he's usually here at this time: but he stays aloof
with the New Latin lot, the Establishment brown nosers
and the like. And ... ah, yes, there he is, Old Sisyphus
always wheeling his trolley to and fro,
loaded to buggery with bottles, cans and rubbish,
and him with asthma and arthritis.
Then the one with a face like Aurora even at midnight,
is Dionysius pulling the corks and silver pumps,
and Ariadne, his reluctant barmaid: she
who ran off with Theseus, an aristo, for a while. But
he was out of her class and she came back, as all
the regulars here knew she would. – But see that thug,

the mug with the scars, well, that's Ajax
quick tempered as a Celt in his cups, and stupid with it.
His mate Achilles also used to come here
but there was this big row with Agamemnon –
him over there with his nose in the air and the silent wife –
and since then Achie (that's what he was known as)
went off in an Olympian-sized huff and hasn't been back
not even when they introduced two meals for a fiver
and a better range of beers from the Fortunate Isles' brewery.
And the guy in the window-seat, stocky sod with restless demeanour,
who's he you'll ask? You'll know him of course: he
was quite famous before he got jailed for fraud –
yes, you've guessed, it's Odysseus. No one knows
what to make of him really. He has a wife
who teaches tapestry at night school, but
she never comes here: a stunner they say
to whom he always returns.
                                    There's plenty more
visit the place, of course, all the Classical in-crowd, as
well as nasty bits of work like Thersites the Spiteful –
got beaten up by Achilles once, but I didn't see it.
Then there are those women, come for the karaoke,
fancy themselves as a pop group, anorexic feminists
who call themselves 'the Muses'.
Also I once saw Helen plain (plain drunk actually),
though some said it was Aphrodite (and have you
seen *her* son? Dreadful child! Thank the gods they don't let kids in here!)
And speaking of the gods – just to round this little monologue off -
give this lot a few glasses of nectar
(Pramnian or Falernian) and by Hades –
yes, he's been here too – a tattooed lout with earrings and no hair –
and, by Hades, Persephone, Cerberus,
everyone claims a hot line to Olympus, Delphi, Dodona, etc.,
giving themselves more airs than
an award-winning poet with a *Consilio Artium cum gratia.**

* Latin for 'an Arts' Council grant'.

The Lost Children

Shadows and windows. Brasses and brown furniture.
A hotel's luxury of past and future –
dry whisperings of the alien, grim-
ness of time. The Pied Piper of Hamelin
spirited the lost children to a nearby
square. Transylvania to live, love and die:
like us all prisoners of music and memory.

Sunk in leather folds of armchair,
nothing to disturb the laden swags of air
nor move one polished leaf of potted plant:
tiny figures of children like soldiers march and chant
along old and decaying streets.
At their shadows history still weeps.

Hotel Bella Musica, Brasov.

The Office Stiff
(a true story)

Always first into work, last out
Joe was the devoted worker
a good respectable guy, gave
no trouble, was never the shirker.

Plugged into his desk thirty years,
a landmark in the office's open plan;
not much noticed by anyone
to the bosses he was 'a solid man',

the ideal employee. Around him desks
were islands with phones that sang like birds;
and bright as day, even at night was
the light in this office of numbers and words.

So bright no shadow could come;
and even when Joe, the respectable guy,
one Monday received his last
phone call and started to die,

the smooth running of the place went on.
Joe just sat there, did not bend,
as the days passed meticulously by
until the cleaners at weekend

noticed him still at his post.
Asked how death could so deceive
his colleagues? Said the boss, 'Oh Joe?
He was always first to arrive, last to leave.'

He was my Prospero

He was my Prospero, my guide
and I think him still alive
somewhere in the undergrowth of silence
that surrounds our life, our dreams.

Where the sad, the sick, find menace,
but others gleam of immeasurable hope,
he is my ghost, indwelling impalpable one
that I choose to live on –
tenant of my darkest dark
a spark of imagined light.

Father, who helped me grow,
lost forever to this dramatic earth,
gave me generous birth,
lacked in himself ego
– like one too wise for it –
but could hand on love –
which is enough, more than enough.

Memory, Snowflakes

How you were once in that high room with me
nonchalant as its dining table that shone
and the fire in its winter grate.
The big old house sleeping in its bones of brick.

Consciously, I didn't rate you then, of course,
just a dad, secure in your crimson jersey
and baggy trousers grey as ash.
Even then, though, my only sparring partner,

I yours, as those late letters between us show.
Recapturing the past in words' strange gleam –
each word a window with sunlight on it –
I realise what a handsome idol you must have been:

as physically good as good-natured, strong,
like one hewn from marble yet warm,
and memory's proof is how all kids loved you.
Well, I'll just sit with you again a moment

of forgotten talk, and together we'll watch snow
flaking and falling outside the window,
hear tall trees creaking at the edge of the lamplit drive
and feel your dead presence with me, still alive,

and I'll think how your thoughts seemed innumerable
as the stars, and ponder how the man of despair
you so often were, transmitted such a love
that even now, years on and gone, you do not leave

but slip back into life not in dream but here
in the ordinary yet evergreen words of poetry.
So that I am humbled into truth and say
something lives, no snowflake melts completely.

Two Oval Portraits Near at Hand

Elizabeth Barrett-Browning brooding
in this tinted photograph
a Mona Lisa without the smile –
pure light within a mind
death's sure darkness under eyes.

Agatha Christie as a child
a far-off picture of her
in far-off Edwardian times –
age of ease and murderous whispers
to disturb, confuse and drive
one little girl wild to solve mysteries.

Sun floods the hotel-terraced hills
of Torquay, in cliffside walks
and gardens floral riches are spent,
tributes to the tourist trade.
Or on other days winter scoops the sea
and wet violence slaps the land.

But all the while words work away
in corners: small money spiders of meaning
expressing what no image can,
                            however near at hand.

The Best Story

A wild sea splatters and batters
the forlorn terrace outside and its tubular steel
chairs. I've read all the stories and still feel,
Christ, there's nothing that betters
yours. The earthy birth in a world of tears
solely consoled by mother and father and
poor creatures in an almost barren land
made up of little harvests and large fears.
Then the life of miracle and generosity,
and never truth so sharply seen,
the flesh transfigured, the godly gleam.
Not in myth before nor subsequent history
such clear forms and sharp lineaments
as your tale. The brutal denouement
followed by resurrection, your light unspent.
No worship, no praise, no compliments
could ever be thanks for the perfection
as son of man you showed the world:
a shocking embodiment of the eternal word,
a peerless knowledge in the midst of corruption.

History

I can see history wherever I turn
in the letters of Hugh MacDiarmid or
the shell-lined grotto of John Scott
of Amwell, patiently, lovingly restored,
shored against blackboard oblivion
by a friend of the world and mine.
It is the unwinding silence in dead people's rooms,
a wind beneath churchyard trees,
the great world snake of perplexity
and the bloom of mind we call poetry.
It is chocolate-coloured snaps in time-foxed tomes
or those 'Way It Was' photographs
in souvenir issues of local papers
(that used to end up as chips-with-history!)
It is what sun scrawls on quartzy walls
and the challenge between tide and stone
that Sophocles lonelily 'heard on the Aegean';
it is the palimpsest left by everyone's dreams
whether of suburban Edens with privet hedges
or mythical Thules 'ringed with bright waters';
and I once saw it, history's river,
Amazon-green and soup-thick rolling between
purple cosmic mountains of sleep.
History, this more than nostalgia,
or seepage of past into present,
is the living dialectic of stones and man,
the long process of discovery of self-in-things
and the unlost memory of every loss
which like stardust falls on our tears.

The Passing of Elizabeth I

The flamboyant tyrant's daughter dying
amidst the mustiness of regal finery:
no keeping back those final minutes flying
towards her last ceremony.

Four-poster bed, velvet drapes, braid –
the best apartment in a willing land
with a fat orange fire servants made.
But to clutch the bellrope her hand

could hardly do. Far off the sounded bell
that summoned Walsingham, Burghley, Cecil
each who'd worn her livery well.
Now, though, a listing vessel

floating towards silence, she can
scarcely keep a lackey's loyal attention.
If she had been a king, a man
would Lord Essex have avoided execution?

One last sigh to give with all the pride
of flags royally swelling in the wind
outside. March 1603. She who'd never bred
children, the glory of an age near blind –

old raddled wreck with thinning hair –
her great staring eyes in shrunken face
beheld a jewel-like vision, a dream,
and smiled at all the ghosts around the place.

Smiled a young girl's smile.
And maid and lady-in-waiting sighed
in unison at that smile, assured greatness
lived on though a queen had died.

The Dispossessed

Yellow child among paddy fields
that became paddy fields of hell,
a girl who fled away a refugee
to be a woman in a land more beautiful
because more safe. A land of
blue lakes and rivers, mountains and
valleys with armfuls of flowers
and undisturbed villages of toy chalets,
and immaculate cities of glass and stone
whose architecture boasted wealth, stability.

Secure and safe in a foreign land
she married, had children of her own,
in time grew old but cared-for –
undoubtedly hers an escape into fortune.
But still, in increase of disquiet,
as the brave new world faded about her
in its fifth, its final season,
the thought of that land first loved
flooded back and choked her mind,
shook her heart with cries of
what might have been and if only
and images from the Book of Life
which is also the Book of Pain,
were leaves and tears of those lost years.

Beyond the Pleasure Principle

The roses of inner rooms, the girls
of cities remind of gardens, streams, flowers,
and their sex falls on me like showers.
Each hand, or breast, or breath moves me:
they light up life explosively –
I feel the sap of spring secrete within
and am swept by love of action and of love.
I see each room, its doors, paintings, plates,
its chairs and coloured carpets, its conversing people,
through a haze of warm blood and wine.

But my friends, city people, diplomats of love
like polished fish, swim in the gilded ripple
seeking ageless satisfactions of wealth
where no satisfaction ever is,
and leave me tormented by the smouldering shells
of their relationships, their private hells.

Spare Some Change?

Platform One, pigeon-grey as all the others
at King's Cross – that cathedral of journeys;
and Gingham's tables and chairs, a spindly
roped-off bistro space, a square retreat
for drink and thought, the best form of waiting:
rumination in a railway station, watching
commuters spill from trains, spread
like suds from an upset pail.
Then, seemingly snug in your retreat,
a few minutes of commodified rest,
'Spare some change?' an ungod bellows,
looms above your seated self: a face to shun
not love, though love it you know you should –
its yellow teeth in fungoid face, its clothes
like a scarecrow's cast-offs
and its desperate glittering eyes ...
But depending on mood (or will –
sometimes you fumble anyway in your cynic's purse)
you give or you don't give. Sometimes, too,
you almost grasp the moral of it:
how and why the needy turn to you
the second you allow your life to stop,
take a break in this decision-driven
money-riven world, take a hard look
at all that's really you.
Your excuse? A cappuccino or a beer,
something to help with the never-quite-knowing.

The Giant

A city is a giant
with long stone careless legs
a cloak
and a squint of sun.

I push these words
to him or it.
Yes, they'll get crunched
beneath feet,

slide like stars to rivers
or wind up
festooned in his beard
with sparrows and pigeons.

London, Paris, N.Y.
all have their own giant
it's where they get
their shadows.

Highest suns and
tallest buildings, domes
and thrones, are swept
by his ruckled cloak,

and his thunder is
behind the messy traffic
of human purpose
another, bigger barbarism.

The Door

Can't quite see through the door,
the small white aperture,
gaze across the parquet floor.
It leads down for sure –
or does it?

Can't quite see through the door.
Guess it opens on a floor
of fallen maple leaves
that sleeve the world in gold,
withered but beautifully old.
Or does it, this door?

This door in suburban Montreal
that maybe leads to the unreal
vision climbing into aero-skies
or even cyberspace.
It is a mathematical door
that one can't see through anymore:
not one of its lovely angles is
quite the same as ours.

But through the doorway of snows
imagination's eye goes
to the grey-glass lake beneath
heavily louring skies.
Geese skitter waters
and planes skim skies –
no small birds are in the murdered grass,
the fiery cardinal and the rest have gone
far to the festive south,
and there's no longer singing here.

For winter is nailed in place
and we can't see through the door
to the real or imagined place.
This open door is like
a pure expressionless face.
Mine or yours.

Colour to the Town

Fogherty wasn't one
        as you'd miss in the least,
for among men and women he was
        'lawless as a beast'.

But for all that, for all
        he was colour to the town,
the snarl and sneer of him
        was lost when they sent him down.

The South Country

'There is no great poetry which can
be dissevered from Nature'
                    Edward Thomas

The Barley Mow, a pub
on the spruced up banks of Thames,
once a Custom's House
now it bears this rural name.
But the Thames here is wide,

wide as a poet's heart; and the river
smell is a sea smell. Clay-
coloured waters, seasoned salt,
that chuckle in stones and mud.

Nearby the Isle of Dogs is a new
Little City: huge phials of glass
filled with specimen humans
obliterating waste land and wharf.
And Limehouse, too, is themed and clean.

The frozen drama of the post-modern
surrounds me.
                    This South Country is changed.
Ineluctably, like a make-over of God.

Two Streams

Twice I fell in love with streams.

The first in the singing
dingle of a wild childhood
where a moor-born flow
entered my mind
dappled and steady and slow.
A stream that pulled at sedge,
foamed yellow sand
and sulked through winters
frozen blind at edges,
or smiled in the quiet sun
of gigantic summers,
sun that fell in shafts
between solemn silver birches.

The second in an Epping vale
where a busy motorway
now is, rambled and ambled
in stone-tugged translucence
through choked cow parsley
and soft mosaics of pink campion
carrying away small shields of leaves
and corn's aftermath shavings,
out of earth and back again –
its water-scents and trepidations,
its under-hedge glitters
linking up with all subtle eternities
and city-bred obscurities
felt in me then, as now.

The Quarry

It was a day of small birds
    and generous skies
they were first shown the quarry.

'My inheritance', were her words.
    It seemed a wise
moment quite lacking the hurry

that characterized that other
    so modern life.
'The farm went to my sister',

she added, her tone that of a mother
    and generous wife.
The larger inheritance had missed her.

He looked about the unkempt quarry
    that yawned at the sun
amid an overgrown and green flurry

of secretive trees, dense-packed.
    A recently begun
dump of cars, abandoned, hi-jacked

or brought there for repair,
    like the ruined Rolls
perfect image of wealthy despair:

two ramshackle sheds having been
    leased to a Mr Bowles,
man in overalls quite unclean.

The quarry a wonder of disuse? Not
      so. Its noontide air was
instinct with plenty, that

green creativity nature gives
      to set against inevitable loss.
Even in the worked-out there lives

something pure like hope –
      the emptiest emptiness
providing always endless scope.

Real Peace

Down all the years I've wanted
a peace: not a cessation of war
nor a foul boredom instead –
foetid air dead in an old jar;

rather a translucent-as-water peace,
peace like the silence of books
or blue endlessness beyond cloud-fleece.
The peace that gives beauty her looks,

makes every flower modeled of light;
is like but is not a snowscape nor
cowslip days of spring, but is in sight
the moment I open a dream door

into the loved orchard of words ...
In a breathless garden where
images and love live and quick birds
flit, beyond reason is real peace then.

A Dream of War

In a night of cold, a purple fever,
I dreamed a dream of war ...

Found myself on a plain of coarse grass
where windy gusts were on the loose
and sea strode into sand-ribbed shore.
What was there? At first unsure
till I saw a splendid city wall
where gilded figures seemed to stroll
or idly lean on parapet and stare:
beautiful women, and old men they were.

At first, I could not see what cried
and shook the air: the dream lied?
Then I saw where those splendid people stared.
Across the bitter plain to where men warred:
shining peacocks in feathery helmets,
their swords hacked and hacked till bodies split
and two small and sinuous rivers
shivered red under wretched willows.

The fight surged back and forth I saw
between the brilliant city and the shore
where wooden ships with coloured sails
tossed like anchored stallions in their stalls,
and spittle-foam, bits of Neptune's beard,
was where green waves cursed and roared.

That city on the plain I knew it then –
tall ladies on the walls and ancient men
watching carnage of the young, bloodlust's boys –
on that plain of dream I witnessed Troy:
the first great European war
to lead to further wars and more.

Tobans

A prison called Outram Road,
such a suburban-sounding name –
Wimbledon or Putney perhaps? –
actually Singapore W.W.2. Very Victorian,
tiers upon tiers of cells climbing up
through rigid silence imposed by
the Japanese – whispering galleries
of despair and hate, no hope.

Two of the guards were, 'Men who appeared
to be English?' An Aussie called Dean
and a Brit name of John O'Malley:
among the first P.O.W.s to come to this
ring of hell with conventional name.
Lackies of a brutal enemy, but
tobans or trusted ones: they helped
feed the prisoners; looked after,
as best they could, the white skeletons that
day after day rattled about or lay
on planks swallowing down sorrow,
madness, pain, anything, with
saucers of weak tea and scrapings of rice.

'I saw O'Malley carry paralysed
men into the sunshine of the exercise yard
in a desperate attempt to keep them alive,
cradling those creatures of skin and bone
in his own emaciated arms ...'

Even in hell the good may be found?
No hope of escape. Nowhere to escape
to. Beatings. Torture. Squalor.
Filthy, rake-thin prisoners of ordure,
odour, sickness-in-and-out. Months
extending to years – months and years
that stank of one thing only: murder.

But even in hell two words reached ears
of the dull and dying: Hiroshima, Nagasaki,
and in a flash of worst history
all was over, all were freed.
But never of the nightmares of memory.

(Lines in quote marks taken from the book
The Railway Man, *Eric Lomax, Vintage 1996.)*

Roses of Picardy

Roses of Picardy are always red
red of the going sun, red of the dawn,
red of the soldiers now long dead –
blood of the roses, blood of the dead.

Thousands and thousands lie in these fields
that fade in the fading light,
thousands who fought and thousands who died
for a cause they were told was right.

Hard to imagine, hard to believe
the fear and carnage that was here
in this landscape of motorways, fields and trees.
Only the lonely moon and its light
only the emptying purple of sky
only the cemeteries' crosses white after white
that number the losses which fed the roses,
the roses of Picardy, petals of the dead.

Thousands and thousands lie in these fields
that fade in the fading light,
thousands who fought and thousands who died
for a cause they believed was right.

No Real Present

It's all a sort of memory,
the good times, the bad –
that perfect meal
oysters, steak, wines of France
like the Marne in sunlight,
lovers in each others' eyes –
always memories.

Today we were in a green village
cows on the easy valley's side
a low-slung inn
the white sky world –
some other mind maybe.

The few convivial hours that pass
their tragic shortness long-felt,
that only art's striving can capture –
there is no real present
only history, mystery, memory.

The present is a slipping away
and all we have is memory
of what or who
is other than ourselves –
the colourfall of fuchsias
in a July garden,
every man and woman going home
elsewhere to some other life

a life not known or seen
like wind, but remembered
sure as touch.

The Wardrobe

An accountant, a poet, an occasional actor –
the last of this strange mixture
led him to a theatre's fitting room
one afternoon of North London gloom.

A top-hat-and-tails, a knight-at-arms,
rows of dresses to show off ladies' charms…
rack on rack of costumes meant
to solve not create bewilderment.

No changing room, just changing then
and there: intermingling women and men,
ghosts seeking to put on character
with all that stored history in dresswear.

The director said, 'Now, let us see…'
and, 'Don't get distracted, just follow me.'
and this was done until there was found
for him a new identity to wrap around

and, as it were, by a kind of game
a different person he became,
like a holy fool or the Dutchman who could fly,
for acting is the world's only legitimate lie.

The Tacit Breeze of Style
(i.m. Anthony Green, artist)

This huge, wood-roofed barn restored
where the Armada's losers, swarthy Spaniards
were imprisoned. Now a cool
sequestered place for tourism and art.
This silent autumn afternoon
I invigilate the paintings of a man
about to die. Carcinoma-flowered, floored,
his self-portrait hung a yard away
from me, and other works, liberal
distributions of colour and limpid line
around the walls. How creative they make
the historic silence of the place
where now the painter's ghost will trawl
this gallery and others I cannot see.
Self-painted like some boxer stripped to the waist,
I rest my eyes on his vivid torso
and face of bearded delicacy, mandarin-like
as some provincial official in Tu Fu's China.
A face without coarseness, almost prayer-fine,
nobly-gentle and gently noble. In bright
pigment and line of flushed silver he speaks
to me, who, in life, spoke only twice with him
in words, and only of inconsequential things.
How did he look just then? I had to say
it to myself, 'Like one surprized by death';
and I was sad to know how true it was,
this present self-portrait, having learned
but an hour before that, having seen this
exhibition of his life's work, he'd left
to close his eyes on Torbay and its sea
and this world's great canvas forever.

Yet the air inside the ancient barn remained creative,
and I was honoured to walk beside him,
glass in hand, through silent, vibrant
landscapes of painting, each fanned
by the tacit breeze of style.

La Joie de Vivre
(Pablo Picasso)

The joy that is sexual not spiritual:
twisted figures in a pastel landscape
yellow and blue and faun-simple.
Joy that is sexual is ultimately spiritual.

Get that pastoral Mallarmé? O!
Did you ever think you'd be so modern?
Cubism and surrealism's Idyll of Joy
this super-sexual eclogue by Picasso.

Is this the remake of Sandro's
La Primavera but with all grace gone?
Proof the gods have not left us alone
who tune these pan-pipes of Pablo's?

Terraza del Caffè
(Vincent Van Gogh)

In this room on a pure white wall
a café framed under splattered stars: stars
like silver droplets round poached egg
planets. The bloodied yellow auberge wall

is tall, cutting into the firework sky.
The café terrace is a wine-red dais
carpeted to honour the visiting vision.
A horse and cart ambles tapping by.

The work of a soul maddened by beauty.
The work of a mind holding infinity.
The work of a dead man out for a drink –
a gone era he vividly felt, we think.

Place du Tertre

Paint-crushed summit of Montmartre
in the solemn, sun-moved shadow
of the grey-white arabesque Sacré Coeur
a swirl of tourists and bistro tables
little trees and bird-sung art-stalls,
mini-galleries amidst mini-trees.
Take coffee, champagne, oysters
in this heady square, aesthete's paradise,
where women's voices tinkle like French bells
and men croon their arguments like Yves Montand.

Here on the singular summit of Paris
where the view is of carved clouds
over rooftops, the Eiffel Tower and
Tivoli, scrunched avenues of sculptured gardens
with blissful fountains and sparrow-filled trees,
Notre Dame and its buttresses stapling
the yellow sunlit sinuosity of the Seine,
its serpent-wind the long glitter of eternity.

Here by the bored swivel of an eye
every life-dweller may pass from Lorrain's
great thoughts of classical distance
to the intimacy of Utrillo or Valadon:
easy as living in a painting, this life
of canvas, contemplation and creativity –
impressionism's cobbled-streeted rain,
cold syllables of pain, or
expressionism's joy companioned by
the glorious jongleur of day, the sun,
where the art of watching's the thing
and heaven's only half in shadow here.

An Artist Contemplates
a Fictional Sketch

You floated into this life,
found yourself there
like a vineyard's angel with black hair
entirely French.

Waiting on a platform for a train's
sprung rhythm from nowhere
to somewhere, the old sun fixing
everywhere with a smile,
and you with your handbag and nonchalance.

It was Bovary Country this
I was sure,
ennui lurked behind water tower
and tasteless garage.
Something had withdrawn itself

from life, mademoiselle, even for
young and beautiful you.
That perfect nose, those quick lips,
eyes trained on distance –
I could draw you without understanding

because we are fellow travellers,
histories that never meet,
sharing only exquisite moments
of profiles, flowers,
and shapes. Shapes of importance
like the ideal *femme*
or crosses in wayside dust.

Rue de Navarin

There could have been a savage burning there too.
No fire escapes, no way down
an inner well of white tiles and a few
patches of struggling ivy. High
in that hotel room one month before
the New York Terror this is what he thought
who'd never thought such things before.

Was it the heat lapping white bodies
in fiery simulacra through the night? Or
dream input to some deeper layer
of world imagination? He couldn't say.
Yet knew 'in event of fire' there'd be no escape.

Next day, quietly reading *Le Figaro*
in the cushioned foyer, insomnia's angst no more
in the safe death of daytime Paris,
he attended to the usual failed prophecies of journalism.

Walking with Words

In Paris, somewhere dawn's dumb pavements,
water hydrants gurgling a fresh day,
and a young woman is a caul of words
as yet unuttered, coming secretly her way.
She's walking, walking with words.

Further off, where leaf-litter blows about
biscuit-coloured banks of the Seine,
an old man shuffles and snuffles along,
in his head last years of joy and pain.
He's walking, walking with words.

O she's a delight that girl, elegant!
He, sadly, could be taken for a tramp.
But for both memory urgent, argent
lights each inner void like a lamp.
They're walking, walking with words.

And it's enough for a poet at his guesswork
to share their hidden, forbidden lives:
a pensive quiver of red lipstick,
an incontinent cough, those wild dropped leaves!
And I'm walking, walking with words.

At the Grave of Baudelaire

Stone-packed acres, pocked toy town
of death, gutted mausoleums,
and you, *mon frère*, for all your renown
shoved in the family tomb
of despised relatives, way off
from where a sculptured figure alone
ponders by the grey graveyard wall.

On your own public cenotaph an angel?
Or is it something of you
looks down at your stone-bandaged corpse,
strange chiselled alter ego
bas-reliefed in heaven or hell?

Thin trees and bushes collect sunlight,
throw doily patterns on death's bric-à-brac
in the cemetery of Montparnasse.
But it does not depress.
For on this day of my long-weddedness,
making this odd pilgrimage
I sense all flowers of evil wither
like the world's infinity of lies –
and much else of which you despaired.

For something goes on of those loved
who have been true, who have cared:
out of the maggot-ridden earth
sweetest thoughts have their birth.

Where the Exiles Dance

The Trocadero fountain brilliantly hushes
the enormous heat painful
as a last wish;
trees too fazed to stir
and the Eiffel Tower
looming like a giant executioner.

Spectator city, city of the mind.

In the old bookshop on the Left Bank
of the medieval river
Seine of intellectual dark and light,
books had a serious air like war –
but a war of ideas
that clash on silent shelves of peace.
Durrell, Joyce, Becket and
all those displaced Americans
Hemingway, Pound, Stein and Miller
who came to this dusty cave,
this deeply platonic shop,
as all must come who care
to know and write and think –
yes, think the unthinkable
where the exiles dance.

Spectator city, city of the mind.

Grey dust of the Louvre Palace
the queue a Kafkaean millepede
shuffling towards the Mona Lisa,
circling under a white sun
a courtyard of columns
and deep dark doorways.

The Arc de Triomphe vast as history,
tawdry places of the Pigalle,
Montmartre that charms by art –
and at every table wine glowing
with the creative feel of Provence,
and words in conversation with images,
and even the legless Utrillo dancing
the dance of exile, miraculous,
in this spectator city, city of the mind.

One heat-crazed August
I, too, came to find what I'd lost,
and dance a little while
the dance of exile.

Reading Proust in Sunlight

The book is somnolent as an old garden
in France, tapestried fleur-de-lis garden,
a golden somewhere that is past now.

Or it is a striped deckchair in lost time
a man or woman reads in, holiday-style,
reads the loving hauteur of a fat book

about the awful Guermantes
or kinky Albertine. But, no,
that's not it, for all the previous magic

leaked by that whingeing aesthetes'
clubman. It is, rather, time's restored
moments of sheer nostalgia

stored in detail. Like now the way's
in sunlight. How a single freckled stone,
a lawn unrolled away to nodding trees,

or tenderly-coloured tended flowers
incarnate romance, things that lose no time
in getting to the heart. Proust's or yours.

Imprisoning Rain

A wonderful heaviness of rain
humming and drumming the roof
hosing down red and blue balconies
while the gulping drain

swallows as quick as it can.
Beneath a no-sky of grey silk
Madame, our elderly neighbour,
comes out at an almost-run

to rescue a prize potted-plant
with feathery white sopping petals,
before scuttling back through shutters.
A poet must just tell it slant

on an afternoon of no-narrative,
trapped by the imprisoning rain.
It is not time for cool beauty
nor the sunlit superlative

but simply waiting for rain to cease:
watching like a cat in a window,
or sheltering down-trodden tramp
or a bird under a useful leaf.

Antibes, Côte d'Azur, 8.12.06.

An Orange Tree

An orange tree breathes over a wall
breathes out silence
ignoring the gabble of street voices
and sky-stitching violence

of jets, needles of pain above.
A fertile orange tree
solemn-sunned and seeding away
beneath this balcony.

Tree heart of a time-chewed town
it gathers to itself birds,
insects, shadows, mystery
and these slow loving words.

Morning in Antibes

Sea hurdles in towards
a bleached fort,
morning in Antibes.

The occasional angelus
clangs the curved
drum of sky, drawing

the indolent mind
back to the idea of heaven.
But this is atheist France

a surly motorist
who knows everything
about this tough old world.

Morning in Antibes,
sunlight brimming
in a champagne glass.

I think the whole world
like this, still yet full
beyond measure:

like the bland sea
between Cap d'Antibes
and the snow-sudded alps

or red shuffled slates
of the old town houses
holding heat like hearts.

Morning in Antibes
beneath this balcony, a
morning forever.

ROOMS

Room 1:   This House

Book-lined spotless dining room
Easter sunlight's silent drumming
of Midas-gold fingers on the table.

Once a study crazy with posters,
books, bottles, bric-à-brac,
where a writer wrote.

Now sea-urged spring laps the window
with new and fertile light where
winter's windy shriek and blare

so recently raged. Now is
only tingling quiet. But her
question comes most sharply in:

'What have you been doing with
your days?' And my answer must be
Remembering!

Remembering the oceanic thoughts and
ripples of feeling that have no shape,
and all the friends who have been here,

explorers looking on another's life –
a written life that is both mine
and hers: my golden poem-maker

and companion of this astounding world

Room 2:   A Collage of Photographs

I have a collage:
        photographs on my wall
that glisten differently in different light
                    like human character.
        She is here, dead centre,
in a large hat at a table on a terrace,
        a sea terrace
the eyeblue-brushed sky luminous as sudden meaning
                    above her.
Here sudden meaning is everything:
        a Japanese fan, a dusty tomahawk,
        a postcard of Chateau Fontenac Quebec,
        St. John's Church Little Gidding,
        Abse at the Pizza Express his 2nd home,
        Nepali poets at Fish Tail Lodge Shangri-la,
        my father at Lulworth Cove, that benign ghost,
        Barker, Donaghy, Caws, Russell – more poets
        challenging life and eternity,
        even a cartoon or two inviting laughter.
A wall display scanned by visitors, passing birds
                all in whatever light.

I have a collage of photos, images, here
        that tell us what we think.
Not everyone may be a poet, painter or musician
        but we are all artists
        of sorts, needing
        to capture the lover,
        hand pushing back hair
on the pier in the wind above salt-sea-spray,
        or a butterfly hovering at
        the mouth of a flower.

Such images I keep of my personal world,
that one day will become like snaps
in the album of God.

Room 3:   4 The Mount

I let myself in by key to spend
a moment in the airy living room
quite empty with its owners away,
and I think of their other home

on fiercely leafy Boar's Hill where
Masefield lived and Irish Yeats visited:
my eyes travelling inward to where
that great poet-contemplative reveried

as I now in this room light as prayer.
Children's parties shrieking with joy recall
and convivial evenings towards the Dartmoor sun,
where valerian crowns the allotment wall

symbolic of the treasures of friendship
in this house, echoingly empty that I love
though it is not mine. If sharing can be said
to be a form of having, then here I surely have?

Have that feeling of belonging to others,
deep in their affections and hearts
so their belongings furnish me with more
of value than what the world thinks is art.

Room 4:   A Kitchen In Cheltenham

Some kitchen! Green, complaisant, Aga-heated
basement that's never cold or damp-defeated.

Room cooked in detail. Marble-topped surfaces,
lectern of food sermons, recipes, oils and spices,

and a long farmhouse table for 12 at least.
A honey-coloured sun spreads its daily yeast

thickly from windows at either end,
though at what time of day it all depends.

An exotic food laboratory where
two reluctant cats sniffily share

their chairs with wine-tasting guests who
in non-culinary mode idly construe

the finer points of creative cooking
simply by the fact of looking:

that vicarious faculty given to man
to experience where he cannot, as if he can.

98

Room 5: Ripon Lodge

Alone in the silence of this splendid room
that, in an hour, will fill with humans partying,
I turn a page of *The Times* that crackles across my knees.
The great window fills with twirling trees
and my eyes having brushed paintings, ornaments,
a piano silent in its elegance, I slip within myself,
down long valleys of mind to meet friends,
mentors, lovers who all argue with destiny...
this passionate destiny that stamps our being,
this wonder of spirit over-wasted in misadventures
and miscalculations made. The rare times
of stillness like now, owed to generous friends, that teach
singular lessons of our failures. Or, rather, just one:
that the dream of life is empty without surrender to vision.
For all is frozen dust, as Hafiz said,
where the Beloved is not. The Beloved
whose face all hope to see in every face.

Room 6:   The Peace

There was a cleverness of intellect hidden
        in that house of bounty.
Its libraried room of window seats
        and green vistas of county.

Fruit lands of Hereford, apple-sweet
        under skies of character.
Birds echoed a furious joy in me
        like some drink-emboldened actor.

A cleverness of intellect that once stormed at me,
        then froze in a twilight photo,
as I saw through walls of happiness
        a host transfigured by ego.

But in heated fields was found forgiveness.
        There where nature's nodding poppies grew
not all the welling anger could suppress
        the generous friendship that I knew.

Walls of happiness. Wells of happiness. Happiness
        with its many golden dusks
spent on evening's terrace talking too much –
        little thinking of the risks

of a too deep questioning in this
        faithless age that's like a cemetery
of despair and minefield of passion.
        Talk that, finally, makes one chary.

On a yellow terrace, content as the perfect
        roses of summer, red bloom

of holy blood, made again happy
in world's greater outdoor room

I could take within a healing
of what sought to drive friendship hence,
and in one inner room again compose
words of praise, words of tolerance.

Room 7:   The Unwinding Room

I came of age in that back dining room
Dutch interior paintings on the walls,
my dad's books like varicoloured columns
either side the fireplace. A back garden's
northern glare through windows, a reedy lake
beyond bushes by the boundary fence,
an Indian or Persian carpet on the floor,
willow-pattern plates, cups and saucers
on the dark wood table
and not-so-comfortable, creaking chairs.

I came of age in that back dining room
a youth moulded at that muddled table
by quarrels with a sister, arguments
with parents who thought they knew
the things that were best for me.

I came of age in that back dining room
atmosphered by tension.
Mother once kicked a coffee table over –

and washed herself from the room
in a flood of tears: and all because
of my sly sister and me.

But in that back dining room I knew
a father ready to talk of any mortal thing
(and immortal, too, though he a non-believer):
a man soaked in Nietzsche and Montaigne who unwound
an intellectual-imaginative curiosity
which has stayed with me, though
the time-shaped days which filled
that room are gone, like my parents and the images
their love collected around my childhood.

I came of age in that back dining room
and have been known to dream of it –
the mind-unwinding room I loved.

Room 8:   A Living Room In Leatherhead

Intimate room, your first flat,
we shared a decade and more ago
before your foreign travels began.
On blow-up beds we lay down
like swathed mummies in winter
or in summer when night sweats ran.
That brief time in Surrey was just
up the hill from the River Mole
which crept behind red houses, under roads,
tugging reeds and roots and flooding grass:
heart-warming days spent visiting pubs
and walking Autumn-tinted woods,

clambering styles, climbing hills.
A time that cannot now return
only be re-run in the movie of Memory:
that place where one grubs out
all lost joys and hidden pain
with, sometimes, a glint of paradise to see.

Room 9:   Penrhyn

That daffodil-and-green drawing room
its ceiling friezed with frozen roses
which bloomed forever in high window light.
It faced an exquisite lawn, often
pearled with mercurial dew,
encircling a great Grecian urn
and linking shade-drenched elms,
chestnuts and the superior oak
with silver-plated birch trees
hemmed in by long-tongued rhododendrons.

Into that room of meditational furniture,
studied cabinets of porcelain,
armchairs, marble fireplace, japonic screen,
books, and printed music sheets
for evenings sung around the piano...
into that drawing room of dreams
flowed the light of childhood.

Light of silk and tapestry's glinting thread
that brightened every image with the power of myth,
then so real, but now unsleeps only
in dreams that unsettle this present world.

Room 10:   Back of the Wool Shop

The setting unlikely you'd have said:
back of a baby clothes' and knitting-wool shop,
on the long road to black Oldham.
Smog-grimed air and life at a seeming stop
now the cotton mills were closing:
the folding away forever of industrial landscape,
though streams and rivers still oozed
effluent, rainbow dyes of no hope.

The setting unlikely I'd have said
for a teenage love affair:
a love that started to be true
for me, and you a girl both serious and fair.
Goodnights under coal-fired stars,
kisses in sodium-frosted streets,
walks in shady parks, journeys in cars,
dances, parties and theatre treats –
love born in an unpromising world. Yet
there had to have been something there
in that sullen district where we first met
and Churchill began his political career.

Room 11:   The Orchid Room

Octagonal glasshouse, conservatory
a mansion's proud projection,
room like a decanter of beauty
filled with floral perfection.

On days of most present light
when exotica's colours multiply,
orchids of supernal design gather
to themselves pure quiet of the lily.

To sit here is to sit in the eye
of a diamond out of which
vein-tongued leaves flame on stems
and grow incredibly flora-rich.

And the tall greenery of garden trees
nod in obeisance to such splendour,
bow to the celebrity status of these
untouchable flowers behind windows.

Room 12: Surreal Room

The thin sunlight of winter London
reaches into the multi-coloured room.
Move and the brown floor creaks,
speaks of feet and many memories
of events held here in past times;
move and the kitchen floor walked is
like a checkered board of bags of crisps.

Electric with self, the moderns sit
in sight of balconies and well-off windows:
people pondering a new and
aimless millennium. Careers bite
and poems follow one another like
streams of carlight across ceilings.
And a black canal slides through London's heart.

Postcards, pens, vased flowers, glass table,
a whole Wailing Wall of medical books
and another of poetry's magical volumes
in eager discourse with little magazines.
Wine bottles dance, whisky dozes,
and so many new ideas check in
to this serious, surreal room.

Room leaning outwards to green squares
of an intimate city where goldfinches
and pigeons talk food and sex
and no one knows whether God exists
save London's Holy Fool, Tom o'Bedlam,
who clambers balconies and laughingly unwinds
his thin scarf of winter sun.

Room 13:   The Much-Married Room

One day you showed us
the pane of glass the burglars broke
to get in. Another time a slate's
neat slice through the conservatory roof
that was part of the 'thirties drawing-room.
Room that whispered 'books' and 'paintings'.
Somehow intellectual, it was
the room of many of our best talks.
Burgundy settee, armless armchairs, chaise-longue,
posies of flowers posing on side tables
and fronded green things in tubs;
the bookcase's white shelves sagged
and sherry-coloured evenings flowed-in
as many a lost sun declined over the garden.
A room of equilibrium in a house
of one of the Muse's much-married couples.
How ever was it possible its sweet life
could be burgled? Or that good partnership
be shattered by a common motor accident?

But it was. And that empty room now lives alone
for all its many friends, its memories.

Room 14:   The Brooklands

Green and gold, green and gold, that's how
               the past there was for me,
and Sid the decorator, George the chauffeur and the
               sadness of World War One
that I inherited, was told so much proudly,
               bitterly about.

Overweight sofas in green moquette, gilded
               leaves round the chandelier,
and those gold-framed oils of far-off country scenes:
               all trees and fields and peasants.
And Sid, a fresh-faced sandy-haired man, grey-flecked,
               promising me:
'When the bugle blows the Hun will rise again
               and then, lad, then
it'll be your turn sure as eggs is eggs!' Solemn exclaimer
               and joker to kids.
Room with an upright piano, custom's shiny cabinets, fine
               period chairs: it gazed
across a terrace, sloping lawn, an unused grassy
               tennis court
and plunged into a garden wilderness where one might
               escape the world.

The Brooklands, three company directors' dwellings,
               that made an odd oasis
in the midst of mills that were asylum-coloured
               and asylum-big
their long bony chimneys like red fingers
               stabbing cloud-belching sky.
Sometimes, when a lemon sun peered peevishly
               through parted fog,

I'd sit on the stone steps out front beside a
flowery urn and think
of great wars, heroes, and a past I would never
be able to visit.

I'd think of Sid the painter and George the chauffeur
and recall the things
my father told me of the Great War, 'That lost
generation,
the finest youth this country ever bred, all dead
in Flanders' mud.'
Sid was a survivor of that war, but Sid said
rude, coarse things.
He came back because he was 'not of the finest'
I concluded after
pondering a long while. Then I'd return indoors
to watch him paint.

Green and gold, green and gold, that's how
the past there was for me.

Room 15:   The Converted Garage

1

Not my home, it was home to me
on and off for a decade:
an orange room, book-invaded.
Somehow blind to the Seventies,
I made it my ground-floor
Ivory Tower where
I would work words after work,
(I was a part-time commuter
and had a 'proper job' then!)
No one drank alcohol
in that house beside a wood:
house loved of suburbia
and kissed by trees, the
sky above threaded by planes
constantly escaping the Heathrow Zoo.
Indoors a house of tired parents,
noisy, teen-cursed but happy.
Yet privacy I had
of sorts: night walks back
through woods watching branches
toss stars into windy skies:
or trudging to Stanmore Station
in snow's white zero weather.
I was young enough then, of course,
for anything, save death
and its powerful nostalgias;
but old enough to long
for those divine coherences
of the imagination: poems.

2

Yes, that orange room: lampshade,
walnut wood shelves, carpet, desk with
inlaid leather top, glowing wallpaper
effusing an amber light
that suffused even thought,
as I struggled with demons
of an unreal separation,
as I wrestled with thoughts
of an equally unreal world, so
much loved, where branches
of a winter wood played shuttlecock
with stars and with my feelings –
those peculiar years I dwelt
in that converted garage.